DINOSAURS AND THEIR DISCOVERERS™

Tyrannosaurus Rex and Barnum Brown

Brooke Hartzog

The Rosen Publishing Group's

PowerKids Press™

New York

Published in 1999 by The Rosen Publishing Group, Inc.
29 East 21st Street, New York, NY 10010

First Edition

Book Design: Danielle Primiceri

Photo Credits: pp. 4, 14, 21, 22 © Linda Hall Library; p. 4 © American Musem of Natural History; p. 6 © Library of Congress/Corbis; p. 7 © Gleason's Pictorial Drawing Room Companion/Corbis; p. 8 Nick Gunderson/Tony Stone Images, Inc.; p. 10 © UPI/Corbis-Bettmann; p. 13 © Hulton Getty/Tony Stone Images, Inc.; p. 17 © 1997 Digital Vision Ltd.

Hartzog, Brooke.
    Tyrannosaurus rex and Barnum Brown / by Brooke Hartzog.
        p.   cm. — (Dinosaurs and their discoverers)
    Includes index.
    Summary: Recounts the life and fossil discoveries of Barnum Brown, the paleontologist who, in 1908, discovered the largest and most complete Tyrannosaurus skeleton that had ever been found.
    ISBN 0-8239-5328-9
    1. Brown, Barnum—Juvenile literature. 2. Paleontologists—United States—Biography—Juvenile literature. 3. Tyrannosaurus rex—Juvenile literature.   [1. Barnum Brown. 2. Paleontologists. 3. Paleontology.] I. Title. II. Series: Hartzog, Brooke. Dinosaurs and their discoverers.
QE707.B77H737 1998
560'.92   98-15383
[B]—DC21   CIP
                                                                                  AC

Manufactured in the United States of America

Contents

The Elegant Explorer

Barnum Brown was a famous **paleontologist** (pay-lee-un-TAH-luh-jist). He became famous when he discovered the world's most complete skeleton of a **tyrannosaurus rex** (tuh-RA-nuh–SOR-us REX) in 1908. All around America, people read about Barnum's adventures in Montana. The pictures of him in newspapers showed an **elegantly** (EH-lih-gint-lee) dressed man. He didn't look much like a person who would like to dig around in the mud and dirt. Even on **digs** (DIGZ) in the middle of the desert, Barnum Brown liked to wear a suit. In fact, he liked ballroom dancing as much as he liked **fossil** (FAH-sul) hunting!

Barnum Brown, all dressed up for a dig, is shown to the right of this twenty-foot ▶ *tyrannosaurus rex skeleton.*

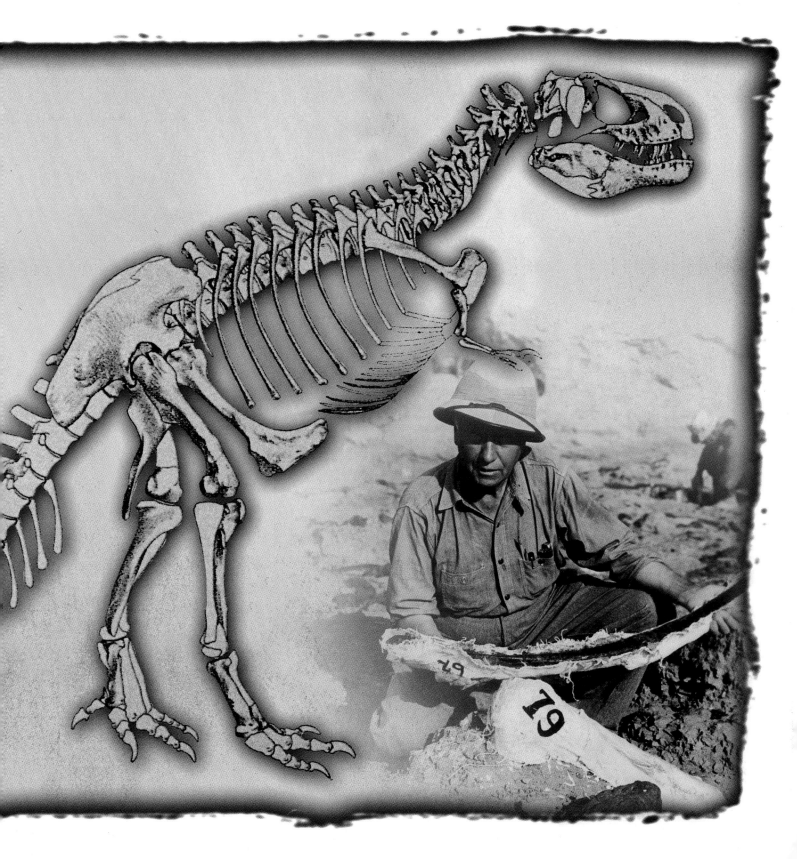

A Star Is Born

   Barnum Brown wasn't always a famous fossil hunter. He was born on his family's farm in Carbondale, Kansas, on February 12, 1873. Around the time he was born, a circus had come through town. Barnum's mother liked P. T. Barnum, the leader of the circus, so much that she named her son after him. Mrs. Brown thought that the name might **inspire** (in-SPYR) her son to become a great and famous man. She was right!

◀ P. T. Barnum's name is still known today because of the Barnum and Bailey Circus, which performs across the United States.

Fossils on the Farm

The Brown family grew crops such as beans and corn on their farm. They also dug up coal and sold it to railroad companies. Railroads burned coal as **fuel** (FYOOL) for steam-powered engines. One day, as he was digging up coal, young Barnum found hundreds of rocks shaped like shells. Millions of years before, the Browns' land had been at the bottom of an ocean. When sea creatures died, their shells and skeletons sank to the bottom, where they were covered with **sediment** (SEH-dih-ment). Over time the sediment became rock. And the remains of these creatures turned into the fossils that Barnum found.

◄ *Barnum found some fish fossils on his land because the land used to be underwater.*

Collecting at College

Barnum went to college at the University of Kansas. He studied paleontology. At college, Barnum learned how to hunt for dinosaur fossils. He went on **expeditions** (EK-spuh-DIH-shuns) with other students and his teachers. He learned that fossils were very **fragile** (FRA-jul). They could easily crumble into a million pieces if he wasn't careful. Barnum studied hard and earned good grades. He got a job with the American Museum of Natural History in New York. If you visit that **museum** (myoo-ZEE-um) today, you will see that many of the most important dinosaur fossils there were found by Barnum Brown.

◄ *Paleontologists handle dinosaur bones very carefully when building exhibits.*

A Nose for Fossils

Barnum's boss at the museum said he thought that Barnum could smell fossils. Of course, no one can really smell fossils that are buried in the earth. But Barnum always seemed to know where fossils were. His fossil-hunting expeditions were like treasure hunts. But the treasure wasn't gold. It was dinosaur bones. He never had a map to help him find fossils. So he had to look for clues that a dinosaur might be buried under the ground.

Paleontologists like Barnum had to spend long hours under the hot sun carefully combing the earth for fossils. ▶

Montana

North Dakota

Idaho

South Dakota

WYOMING

Apatosaurus and allosaurus fossils have been found in some parts of Wyoming.

A House Made of Bones

While searching for fossils in Wyoming in 1898, Barnum heard about a strange hut that was nearby. A shepherd had built the hut out of bones. Barnum went to **investigate** (in-VEH-stih-gayt) and found the bone cabin in a valley. There were thousands of bones just lying around the valley. The bones were dinosaur fossils. Barnum and his helpers set up camp there and called it "Bone Cabin Quarry." They **excavated** (EK-skuh-vay-ted) skeletons of many **Jurassic** (jer-A-sik) dinosaurs, such as the **allosaurus** (a-luh-SOR-us) and the **apatosaurus** (uh-pa-tuh-SOR-us).

Life on an Expedition

Finding dinosaur fossils was not always easy. The places where fossils are found are often **remote** (rih-MOHT) areas, such as canyons and deserts. Deserts can be hot during the day and very cold at night. There weren't any hotels in deserts, so Barnum Brown and other fossil hunters had to camp out in tents. They had to hunt animals, such as antelope, or catch fish for food. They often spent whole days searching for water in the hot desert.

Somehow Barnum knew where to look in a big desert to find fossils. ▶

16

Fossils Far and Wide

CUBA

Barnum Brown traveled all over the world in search of fossils. Sometimes he **explored** (ek-SPLORD) for two long years before coming back home. He once flew a shaky airplane over deserts in search of clues. He fought robbers in India. Once, he even swam into an underground stream in search of fossils in Cuba. But no matter what he was doing, Barnum

INDIA

always
dressed as
if he were
going out to dinner rather
than digging for dinosaurs in
the deserts.

◄ *Fossil hunters have to travel all over the world to gather different types of dinosaur bones.*

Famous Finds

In 1908, Barnum Brown made his most famous discovery in Hell Creek, Montana. He had been looking for clues for a month without finding a single bone. He was about give up, but he decided he would search for one more day. On that very day, Barnum found the biggest and most complete tyrannosaurus rex skeleton that had ever been discovered. It was bigger than a train car! Getting it back to the museum wouldn't be easy.

Barnum and his helpers spent two summers trying to excavate the huge tyrannosaurus bones from the rocks. They had to blast out the rock around the biggest bones with **dynamite** (DY-nuh-myt).

Tyrannosaurus rex was a huge dinosaur that scientists believe was 46 feet long and 18 feet tall. ▶

Moving the Skeleton

There weren't any cars in the early 1900s. So Barnum and his helpers had to load the giant skeleton piece by piece onto horse-drawn wagons. The **pelvis** (PEL-vis) bones of the dinosaur weighed as much as an elephant. They had to be moved on a specially built sled pulled by four horses. The sled had to be dragged almost a hundred miles to the nearest train station. But no matter what challenges he faced, Barnum Brown worked hard and never gave up!

Glossary

allosaurus (a-luh-SOR-us) A huge meat-eating dinosaur found in North America in the Jurassic period.

apatosaurus (uh-pa-tuh-SOR-us) A Jurassic dinosaur also known as a brontosaurus.

dig (DIG) When people go on a search to dig for dinosaur bones.

dynamite (DY-nuh-myt) Something used to blow things up.

elegantly (EH-lih-gint-lee) Beautifully and neatly.

excavate (EK-skuh-vayt) To dig up something that was buried or covered by rocks.

expedition (EK-spuh-DIH-shun) A trip people take to find out more about something.

explore (ek-SPLOR) To search for something.

fossil (FAH-sul) Remains of an animal or plant from the past, found in Earth's crust.

fragile (FRA-jul) When something can break very easily.

fuel (FYOOL) A source of heat or energy.

inspire (in-SPYR) To make someone want to do something.

investigate (in-VEH-stih-gayt) To try to learn the facts about something.

Jurassic (jer-A-sik) A period in history during the Mesozoic era, which is when the dinosaurs lived.

museum (myoo-ZEE-um) A building where historical items are displayed.

paleontologist (pay-lee-un-TAH-luh-jist) Someone who studies things that lived in the past, such as dinosaurs.

pelvis (PEL-vis) The hipbones.

remote (rih-MOHT) Something far away from anywhere that humans live.

sediment (SEH-dih-ment) Gravel, sand, silt, or mud that is carried by wind or water.

tyrannosaurus rex (tuh-RA-nuh-SOR-us REX) A huge two-footed, meat-eating dinosaur that lived in North America during the Upper Cretaceous period.

Index